23.95

RC
628
S8
2007

Fat in America

by Gail B. Stewart

ERICKSON PRESS

Yankton, South Dakota

ERICKSON PRESS

© 2007 Erickson Press

For more information, contact
Erickson Press
329 Broadway
PO Box 33
Yankton, SD 57078

Or you can visit our Internet site at www.ericksonpress.com

Library of Congress Control Number: 2007920458
ISBN 978-1-60217-002-5

Contents

A Land of Fat People

Rusty is a Minnesota thirteen-year-old. He says that he is the heaviest kid in his middle school. The average weight for boys his age is 100 pounds (45kg). "I weigh 204 pounds," he says. "I'm too fat. I can't do sports. I'm not good at stuff like that."

Rusty does not like to talk about his weight. He says his mother tells him every day that he is too heavy. He hears the same thing from kids at school. He wishes everyone would leave him alone.

"I don't like being fat," he says. "But I don't want to go on a diet, either. I'd hate eating diet food. I don't like fruits and vegetables. Fruit is okay if it's in a pie, but not just by itself. But for dinner, I like hamburgers and stuff like that. I like McDonalds, and I like when we order pizza. I told my mom no way am I eating salads. I'd rather just stay fat."[1]

One Wish

Jillian understands how Rusty feels. She is fifteen and lives in Oklahoma City. Like Rusty, she weighs too much.

"I don't want to say what I weigh," she says. "It's my business, you know? I know it's too much. But everybody thinks they have to tell you you're fat. Don't they think I know? Don't they think I have a mirror? I just hate it. My mom says, 'How about an orange?' or 'Wouldn't a salad be good?' What she means is 'Boy, Jillian, you're really fat.'"

An overweight teen sits alone in the school gym.

Jillian admits she thinks about being thin every day. She says:

If I had one wish, I'd wish I was skinny, skinny, skinny. I'd wear jeans like everybody else. I'd be able to tuck in my shirt. I could eat anything I wanted. And have desserts

An overweight girl checks her appearance.

without worrying about getting heavier. And people wouldn't refer to me as "that fat girl."

But it's really hard to get thin. I envy people who are thin. They don't even think about what they eat. They could eat pizza or ice cream every day. But I try to slim down. I have been on lots of diets. But nothing really works for me. I'm just born to be fat, I guess.[2]

An American Epidemic

Rusty and Jillian are not alone. There are 9 million overweight children and teens in the United States. Another 16 million are close to being overweight. More and more young people are obese, or severely overweight. The numbers are growing every year. Since 1985 the percentage of overweight children has doubled.

The rate of overweight adult Americans is even worse. Two-thirds are overweight or obese. That is 130 million people. That number is increasing rapidly, too. Doctors say that such numbers make obesity an epidemic.

Being fat is a dangerous health risk. It affects a person's heart and lungs. It affects bones and muscles. Being overweight can have deadly consequences. It can cause a number of life-threatening diseases. In 2005 almost half a million Americans died because they were too fat. Soon being overweight will kill more Americans than smoking does.

Adult Obesity in America
Average for 2003–2005

In 14 states, over 25 percent of adults are obese.
Obesity is a major health problem in the United States.

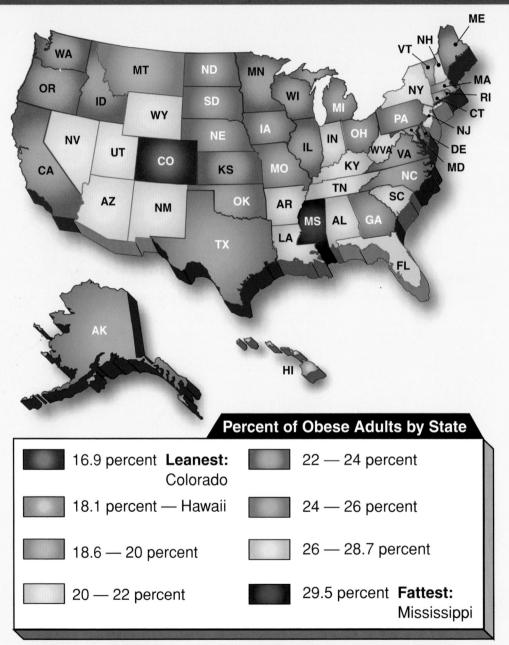

Percent of Obese Adults by State

16.9 percent **Leanest:** Colorado		22 — 24 percent	
18.1 percent — Hawaii		24 — 26 percent	
18.6 — 20 percent		26 — 28.7 percent	
20 — 22 percent		29.5 percent **Fattest:** Mississippi	

Sources: http://calorielab.com. Three-year average from 2003–2005. In Hawaii, data not collected in 2004; average is based on 2003 and 2005 data. / CDC, Behavioral Risk Factor Surveillance System database.

A girl and her mother try to stay fit by doing yoga.

Connie is a pediatric nurse. She sees many overweight children every day. She says:

Really, I think about it all the time. We've never had this many overweight Americans. Every day we see them here, in the clinic. Especially kids—this is a new thing. It's terribly sad, and terribly dangerous, too. Being overweight hurts young people. It makes them unhealthy. And it makes them feel alone and different from other kids. We've got to wake up. This is a real crisis.[3]

Chapter 1

How Did America Get So Fat?

A century ago, an overweight child was a rare sight. There were far fewer overweight adults, too. What has changed to make people fatter? Doctors have studied how people used to live. They looked at the kind of foods people ate. They looked at the type of exercise people used to get. What doctors learned explained everything.

No Exercise

One thing that has changed over the years is exercise. People are not as active as they used to be. Today they use elevators instead of stairs. They drive instead of walk. Their bodies do not burn as many calories. As a result, they pack on pounds.

Bill works in a weight-loss center in Minnesota. He talks to a lot of overweight people each day. He says:

A hundred years ago few people were overweight.

They come in because they want to be thin. I start by asking them what exercise they get each day. Most of them shake their heads. They act like I'm speaking another language.

I ask them if they walk the dog. I say, "Do you swim? Do you do yard work? Do you go dancing?" But really, most of them say no to everything. They just don't exercise.

Some people get exercise by walking to shops or to work.

He says that he notices one thing about most of his clients. People depend too much on driving. "Nobody walks," he says. "If people would do a couple of errands each week on foot, they'd lose weight. But walking isn't part of the American lifestyle."[4]

Jeri, a teacher's aide, agrees. She moved to Saint Paul from a rural town. She says:

We lived way out in the country. Our farm was six miles from town. We needed our car for everything. When we moved here, I was excited. Our new neighborhood is close to everything! There is a library four blocks away. A little grocery store two blocks away. I thought I'd walk everywhere. But I don't. I drive. Sometimes I say that it's because of the cold. Or because I'm in a hurry. But really, it's just that I have become lazy. I depend on my car too much. Some habits are hard to break, I guess.[5]

Indoor Childhood

Experts are most worried about young people. Children and teens do not get enough exercise, either. That surprises many adults. They remember being active when they were young. Martin is an

Many teens prefer video games to physical activity.

Kids fear playing outside in neighborhoods with high crime rates.

example. He is a father of nine-year-old twin boys. He is worried that his sons are not more active.

"When I was a kid, we all played," he says. "After school, kids hit the park, the playground, whatever. We played ball. We rode our bikes. We ran around. It was fun after sitting in school all day. We couldn't wait to get outside. My mom had trouble getting us inside at dinnertime. And after dinner, we'd beg to go back out."

Martin says he has to force his sons to go outdoors. "They'd rather be watching TV," he says. "Or playing Nintendo. Or even sitting at the computer. I guess anything with a screen. I don't object to those things. But they are missing out. A lot of kids are. I can't understand why they would rather sit!"[6]

But there are other reasons children stay inside. Many do not live in safe neighborhoods. Their parents do not want them outside without an adult. Trina lives in Minneapolis. She has three children. She is one of these parents. She says:

> We live on the north side of the city. There is a park only a block from our house. It's easy walking distance. But there are older kids there. There are some who sell drugs. They fight and get into trouble. Every day

Food Deserts

Researchers are looking at another cause of obesity. They call it a "food desert." This is a part of a city with no grocery stores. There may be corner stores. But these have no fresh vegetables or fruit. The food is not as healthy. Food deserts do have lots and lots of fast food restaurants. These are not very healthy, either. This is one reason many people in food deserts are fat.

In Chicago, many neighborhoods on the south and west sides are food deserts. Chatham and Roseland are two examples. These neighborhoods are mostly poor. People who live there might have trouble getting to a real grocery store. Many poor people do not own a car. They must sometimes travel an hour by bus to a store. Getting back home is even harder. They have many heavy bags of groceries. Many who live in the food deserts do not bother with the long trip. It is just easier to eat fast food instead.

there's sirens. Police are always getting called over there.

My kids would love to play outside. But I won't let them. It's me, not them. I want them home. I bought them video games so they don't complain. But that park? In our neighborhood, it's just not safe.[7]

No Help from Schools

Most young people no longer get exercise in school, either. For many years schools helped them keep fit. Several times each week students attended physical education classes, or P.E. They

Boys gather for P.E. class. Many schools no longer have P.E.

did exercises. They also learned a wide range of sports and games. Even if their neighborhoods were unsafe, students were active in school.

But many schools no longer offer P.E. classes. They began dropping them in the mid-1990s. School boards wanted more money spent on classroom teaching. They urged schools to cut P.E. Many board members felt such classes were a waste of time. "If you have P.E.," said one Texas board member, "you can have kids that are healthy and dumb."[8]

Other experts did not agree. Dr. David Satcher was the U.S. surgeon general in 2004. He said it was important for people to be active early in life. That way they would have a better chance of being active adults. That is an important lesson for schools to teach. Satcher said, "Our schools have a responsibility to educate both minds and bodies."[9]

A Bigger Problem

But lack of exercise is only part of the problem. Food is an even bigger issue. Bill works as a weight-loss counselor. He says his clients make poor choices about the food they eat. "Food is a huge problem," he says. "We are eating too much. We eat the wrong kinds of food. And it's making us fat."

Fast food is a growing problem. The kinds of food served in restaurants like McDonald's is tasty and cheap. However, it is loaded with fat and calories. "It's my favorite food in the world," Bill admits. "Burgers and french fries are the best. But

All in the Family

Being fat sometimes runs in families. Some parents eat too much. They do not exercise. They may teach their children those bad habits. Sometimes these parents are confused about how to help their children. Alyssa's parents are like that. She is five. She already weighs 90 pounds. Her mother says, "I don't have control over my own eating. How am I supposed to teach my daughter?" The doctor says Alyssa will do better if her whole family works together. They can exercise together. They can eat the same healthy foods. The doctor says, "The whole family has to develop healthier lifestyles."

Jill Smolowe, "Everything to Lose," *People.* November 4, 2002, p. 58.

Kids of overweight parents may also have weight problems.

I've got to resist. I know it isn't good for me. That kind of food has too many calories. Too much salt. Way too much fat and added sugars."[10]

Too many families today rely on fast food. In 1977 only one meal in ten was from a drive-through. In 2005 it was one meal in four. "For me it's cheap," says Trina. "I have three kids. I'm on a budget. I can feed them from Burger King for under twelve dollars. I couldn't afford to take them to a restaurant. Plus, my kids love the food. They'd eat takeout every day if I'd let them."[11]

Meals at fast food restaurants can be full of fat.

Too Much Food?

The size of portions is another problem. Restaurants are making servings larger. People want to feel as though they are getting more for their money. So restaurants increase the portions. A standard helping of meat is 6 ounces (170g). But many restaurants give customers a 12-ounce serving (340g), or even larger. A standard serving of pasta is a cup (227g). But most restaurants heap two or three cups (454 to 680g) on the plate.

"That's what people expect," says Gavin. He runs a restaurant in a Chicago suburb. "If we gave people what restaurants used to serve, they'd get mad. They'd think we were cheating them. People are used to full plates. And our plates are bigger than they were in 1990!"[12]

Restaurant meals have 60 percent more calories than home-cooked meals. And Americans are eating out more than ever. In 2005 one-fourth of people's meals were from restaurants. People are getting too many extra calories. This means more overweight families.

Portion sizes at restaurants are getting larger.

Not Just Restaurants

It is not just restaurant servings that are too big. The portions of many convenience foods have grown, too. A regular candy bar is two-thirds larger than the same candy in 1978. A single small bag of potato chips is larger, too. There are about twenty more chips per bag than in 1978. Movie popcorn is also a much bigger serving today. In 1956 an order was about 3 cups (680g). In 2006 a single order was 16 cups (3,629g).

The biggest change is soda pop. People are drinking more soda than ever before. Mac is a father of two teenage boys. He says he is amazed at how much soda they drink. "When I was a kid, my parents were strict about it. One pop a day, if at all," he says. "And the bottles were tiny! Six and a half ounces. Today, a bottle of pop is twenty ounces. And many kids drink several a day."[13]

Movie popcorn containers range from small to huge.

Soda is a problem because it contains nothing healthy. There are no vitamins or minerals. "It tastes good, and that's about it," says Bill. "But like most junk food, it cheats your body. It makes you feel full. And when you're full, you don't eat foods that are healthy for you. And that can lead to real trouble."[14]

Chapter 2

The Dangers of Being Fat

Being fat causes a number of problems. Some are annoying, such as having clothes that are too tight. That is what doctors call a cosmetic problem. It has only to do with appearances. But there are other problems that are more serious. Having extra weight can be dangerous to a person's health.

Who Is Fat?

There are tools for deciding if someone is too heavy. Many doctors use a special chart. The chart shows different columns. Various heights and weights are listed. Each column has a number.

A person's height and weight will have a number. That number is called the body mass index, or BMI. There is one chart for children. There is one for men and women, too. The BMI number can show if someone is overweight or obese. Usually a person with a BMI above 30 is obese. Between 25 and 29 is considered overweight.

How to Calculate Body Mass Index (BMI)

BMI is a calculation that uses a person's height and weight to estimate how much body fat that person has.

The BMI calculations for a teen, Jane, are shown below. Jane is 15 years old, 5 feet tall, and weighs 150 pounds.

1. Enter Jane's height in inches:
One foot = 12 inches
For Jane, 5 feet x 12 inches = 60 inches

60 inches

2. Multiply her height in inches by itself:
60 x 60 = 3600

3600

3. Enter Jane's weight in pounds:

150

4. Divide her weight by the answer in Line 2:
150 pounds ÷ 3600 = .0417

.0417

5. Multiply the answer in Line 4 by 703:
.0417 x 703 = 29.3

29.3 This is Jane's BMI. She may be overweight.

Find Out Your Own BMI Online

Teens grow quickly, so their BMI may vary from month to month.

This is why an online BMI calculator will ask for your age.

You will find a BMI calculator at this Web page:
http://apps.nccd.cdc.gov/dnpabmi/Calculator.aspx

Follow the instructions to learn your BMI and to find out what it means.

Source: Centers for Disease Control and Prevention.
For more information, see the Appendix, page 59.

Experts say the BMI is good because it is based on height, too. "Take a man who is 6 feet 4 inches and another man who is only 5 feet 5 inches tall," says Bill. "They could both weigh 180 pounds. The tall man would not be overweight. His BMI would be 22. But the short man's BMI would be 30. That would make him obese."[15]

Bones and Joints

Rusty, age thirteen, weighs 204 pounds (92.5kg). One thing his doctor told him was to get more exercise. "But I can't," admits Rusty. "It's hard for me to run. Some days it's even hard to walk."

Rusty has problems with his joints. His knees and hips are especially sore. Many overweight people have the same problem. There is a cushion in a person's joints called cartilage. It keeps the bones from grinding together. But when someone is fat, there is too much pressure on the cartilage. It soon wears down. It cannot provide a good cushion. When this happens, the joints become painful.

"It's a kind of arthritis," Rusty explains. "It seems weird to have arthritis when you're thirteen. But it's because of my weight. It mostly hurts my knees. They ache, just really hurt bad. The bones kind of click together. I can hear them. But sometimes my hips hurt, too—especially during the night. It's hard to sleep. But then when I get up, that's hard, too."[16]

Dangerous Sleep

Another physical problem happens during sleep. It is called sleep apnea. Apnea means "without breath." People with sleep apnea actually stop breathing while they are asleep. They may stop for

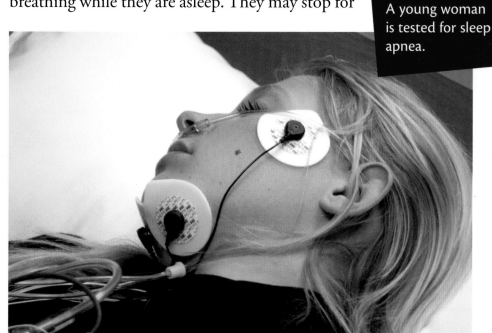

A young woman is tested for sleep apnea.

a few seconds. Sometimes they stop for one or two minutes. During that time they struggle. They gasp as they fight for air. Then they awaken for a few seconds and breathe. Afterward they fall back asleep. This can happen hundreds of times during a single night. They do not remember waking up during the night. They do not realize their breathing stops.

Most cases happen when the airway in the throat is blocked. Fat people carry weight in their faces and necks. When they sleep this extra weight puts pressure on the airway. Then the airway closes. That makes the person gasp for air. Anyone can have sleep apnea. But someone who is fat is five times more likely to have it. And more and more overweight teens are being diagnosed with it, too.

People with sleep apnea may fall asleep at work.

Super-Sized Caskets

Many items are bigger today. This is because there are more fat people. There are special seat belts in airplanes. There are car seats made for overweight toddlers. And there are extra-large caskets, too. A casket company in Indiana makes them. Regular caskets are 24 inches (61cm) wide. The new super-sized ones are 44 inches (112cm) across. They also have stronger hinges and handles. They can handle a 700-pound body (318kg).

Business is booming. In 1980 the company sold only about one each year. But today there is more demand. They sell five each month.

Sleep apnea is dangerous for two reasons. First, people get less sleep. Waking up over and over to breathe is not restful. It does not allow them to get deep sleep. When that happens they are tired the next day. They may doze off at work. They may even fall asleep driving.

The other danger is damage to the heart. Gasping for breath is hard on the body. The heart has to pump harder. This can lead to heart damage. The heart may pump in an irregular rhythm. This could even cause a heart attack or a stroke.

Heart Problems

The heart suffers in other ways, too. Blood supplies the body with oxygen and other things to

Teens attend a weight-loss camp.

keep it healthy. A bigger body means more blood is needed. And more blood means that the heart must work much harder.

The heart is a muscle. It gets larger the harder it works. Over time, the heart becomes too big. It eventually stops. Obese people are ten times more likely to have such problems. Experts worry because more children and teens are showing signs of heart trouble, too.

Connie is a pediatric nurse. She works in a clinic where there are many heavy patients. "We have seen children as young as ten or twelve who have heart problems," she says. "They weigh more than an adult man should weigh. They can only walk a few steps before sitting down. They are always out of breath. Their hearts just can't keep up."[17]

Diabetes

Another serious problem for fat people is diabetes. Diabetes is a very dangerous illness. It prevents a person's body from changing food into energy. A healthy body turns food into a sugar called glucose. The cells of the body use glucose as fuel. But each cell has a tough wall around it. The glucose has to get through the cell wall. So the body makes a special chemical called insulin. Insulin acts as a key. It helps the glucose get past the tough cell walls.

The cell walls of a fat person are also covered with fat. This makes them even tougher. The insulin cannot help the glucose get through the cell walls. When that happens, the glucose stays in

Sugar Everywhere

Americans eat more sugar than any other people. They have between 20 and 33 teaspoons each day. That number surprises people. They do not think they eat that much sugar. A lot of the sugar is in soda. Americans drink a lot of soda. But sugar is added to many other foods. There is sugar in pizza and bread. It is in hot dogs, soup, and crackers. It is added to canned vegetables and ketchup. It is in mayonnaise and lunch meat. These foods do not taste sweet but they have added sugar. And all of this sugar is one big reason why Americans gain weight.

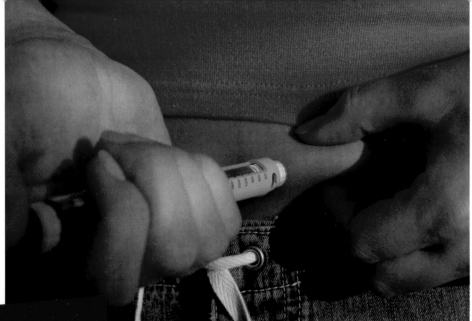

the blood. The cells become weak because they have no fuel.

More Problems

The buildup of glucose in the blood is dangerous. Too much glucose makes the blood thick. Thick blood cannot move through some tiny blood vessels. When blood is too thick it can cause blood vessels to burst.

Another problem is nerve damage. Heavy people with diabetes can lose feeling in parts of their bodies. That is a big problem. Nerves tell people when they are hurt. Connie is a nurse. She says, "If you cut yourself, your nerves tell you. But when you are numb, you don't know when you are hurt."

Connie worked with a heavy thirteen-year-old girl. She had diabetes and nerve damage. The girl had stepped on a nail. She did not even feel it. The wound became infected. It was so infected that it would not heal. "The doctors had to amputate two toes," says Connie. "Any amputation is sad. But for a child—that's about as bad as it gets."[18]

"A Sad Fact"

Scientists continue to study obesity. They are learning more every day. One new worry is the link between obesity and cancer. They have found that fat people are more at risk for certain cancers. Colon cancer is one of these. Breast cancer is more common in heavy women. Doctors are not yet sure why.

One thing doctors do know for sure is that obesity is dangerous. Rob Larson is a Minnesota doctor. "I'm very, very troubled about overweight kids," he says. "We see far too many these days. They face so many health problems. If they stay heavy, things will get worse. They are looking at a future of poor health. It's a sad fact."[19]

A young man is tested for health problems caused by his obesity.

Chapter 3

Fat on the Inside

Being overweight can cause great physical problems. But there are other problems that are just as serious. They can cause the person to feel lonely or sad. They can cause frustration and anger. These problems can lead to depression, too.

Corrine is a very heavy fifteen-year-old girl. She says people do not understand her. "People know I'm fat," she says. "That's obvious. I've always been fat, since I was a little girl. But people don't know what I feel like inside. Not even my family. Everybody just sees me as a fat girl."

Corrine says she feels cut off from other people. "I feel really different from them," she says. "I feel like they are from one planet and I'm from another. They don't know what it's like. They don't know how it feels to look like me. See, for me, being fat isn't just how I look. It's also my emotions. It's like the fat is inside me, too."

Making Judgments

People often make judgments about people who are fat. They say such people are sloppy or lazy. "Most people have wrong ideas," says Corrine. "They act like I sit around all day eating candy. Or ice cream out of the carton. But I don't do those things."

She also says people believe she chooses to be fat. "Like I would do that," she says. "I hate how I look. I hate wearing baggy clothes. I hate wearing 4X men's sweatshirts. Why do people think I like being like this?"[20]

Debbie is a seventeen-year-old girl from Wisconsin. She admits she thinks some of those things about fat people. "When I see a fat person, I am grossed out," she says. "I feel like, okay, you chose to be fat. No one forces you to eat. Maybe I am too judgmental. But it seems like the fat kids just don't care how they look. I don't get that."

Heavy people may feel embarrassed by their size.

She says she knows some people cannot help it. "There's a girl in my high school who is heavy," she says. "But she is on some medication. It makes her face fat. She wasn't like that before. So I figure, it's not like she ate a million doughnuts. She's got an excuse."[21]

Debbie is not alone. A lot of people have negative judgments about fat people. Scientists have

Most overweight people do not like being heavy.

done studies about such judgments. They find that negative ideas start at a very early age. In one study, scientists talked to preschool children. They showed the children pictures of many young children. One picture showed a chubby child. The preschoolers said that child must be "meaner, stupider, louder, and sloppier"[22] than the others. Only 16 percent said they would be friends with a chubby child.

No Surprise

Adults make similar judgments about fat people. Researchers did a study with college students. They asked what sorts of traits the students would accept in a date. They gave choices of many traits. Some were physical, such as bad teeth or a limp. Others traits were about personality. The results showed that few would consider dating a fat person. In fact, more would rather go out with a drug user. Some said they would rather date a criminal than a fat person.

Fat people face discrimination getting jobs, too. Valerie is a good example of this. She is very smart. She has a master's degree in computer engineering. She talked to an employment agent on the phone. She wanted to get a good job. The man was excited when he heard how qualified Valerie is. He told her, "I can get you any job you want."

But he changed his mind when he met Valerie in person. Valerie weighs almost 400 pounds (181kg). The man said, "You're too fat to sell."[23] He told her she probably would never get a good job.

Two people wait for job interviews. Looks can affect chances of getting a job.

Raging Bull

Michael is a young Chicago man. He weighed 300 pounds (136kg) when he was in high school. He had a very public embarrassing moment. It happened at a Six Flags amusement park. He was with a girl he liked. They decided to ride a scary roller coaster called Raging Bull. But the bar on the seat would not fit around him. The ride worker told him he was too fat for the ride. Everyone laughed as he climbed down.

Michael vowed then he would get thinner. He told himself, "That's it, I'm done with this fat stuff." He began going to the gym. He was too fat to do much at first. Sometimes he felt like staying home. But then he would remember the Raging Bull. "Then I always made it," he says.

Quoted in *Men's Fitness*, "Too Wide to Ride." August 2004, p. 78.

Valerie's story is familiar to thousands of other heavy people. The Chicago Medical School decided to do an experiment. Researchers wanted to see how often discrimination happens. They had actors make a videotape of themselves. In the videotapes they talked about getting a job. They told their education and experience. After making the videotapes the actors made new videos. In the new ones they disguised themselves. They wore special suits that made them look very fat. But their words were very similar.

Employers were asked to view the tapes. A researcher asked who they would hire for the job.

The results were not surprising. The thinner people got the job. No one wanted to hire the fat person.

"Fair Game"

For fat people there are always reminders of being different. These are very hard on children and teens. Raechel, an Oklahoma teen, agrees. She

A make-up artist shows parts of a fat suit he designed.

Overweight teens may have few friends at school.

weighs 323 pounds (146.5kg). She says her class-mates have always teased her. She tried every diet. But nothing worked. She says, "It's horrible to be heavy."[24]

"Fat kids are a target," says one girl, who asked not to be named. "Even kids who seem nice make fun of you if you're fat. It's like no one really thinks it's cruel. They'd never make fun of a retarded kid. Or one who is blind or something. But boy, if you're fat, you're fair game." She has had people moo when she walks down the hall in school. "Even the girls do it," she says. "It makes me hate school. I wish my mom would let me stay home."[25]

Being mocked and taunted is hard. Many fat teens withdraw. They do not want to call attention to themselves. Jillian is an overweight Oklahoma high school student. She explains:

> You can get really quiet. You hope no one notices you. Or you just leave the room. I did that a lot, even when I was in grade school. The teacher might be reading a story out loud. If there was a whale or a pig in it, I knew I had to get out. Otherwise, when [the teacher] got to that part, the kids would turn around and laugh at me. Like I was the pig, you know? So I'd try to leave. I'd ask to go to the nurse.

> The worst time was third grade. The teacher read *Charlotte's Web*. That's the one with the pig and the spider. I hated it. I just put my head down on my desk. I didn't want to look up. I knew they were looking at me. I still hate that book.[26]

A Different Strategy

Some fat teens try something different. They make fun of themselves before others can. Michael remembers doing that. He was the heaviest student in his Chicago junior high school. He weighed 200 pounds (90.7kg).

He especially hated gym class. He could not do exercises. He was not good at sports. Michael says he really dreaded the fitness tests each year. "I

knew those tests would embarrass me," he says. He tried making fun of himself. He would say, "Fat kids can't do pull-ups."[27]

But his jokes backfired. The other students laughed. But they laughed at him, not with him. They called him names like Shamu and Blubber-Butt. The experience was like torture for him.

Isolated

Such experiences make fat children feel left out. They feel as though they have no value. And those feelings create problems, too. Some get depressed. Others get angry. Sharri is a twelve-year-old girl. She gets teased because she is very heavy.

She says she gets mad, but at the wrong people. Sharri says:

> I yell at my family. I don't say anything to the kids at school. I guess I'm afraid of them. They say really mean things. Or they talk about me—and I'm sitting right there! That's so mean.

> I don't tell the teacher when that happens. That's what my mom would tell me to do. But then the kids would hate me more. So

Often lonely, overweight teens may be depressed and angry.

Super-Size the Mac and Cheese

Experts say that people eat more when they are served large portions. It does not matter if the person is hungry or not. At the University of Pennsylvania, researchers did an experiment. They served helpings of macaroni and cheese to a test group of young men. On the first day, the men were served 16 ounces. They ate 10 ounces. The next day they were given a larger portion. It was 25 ounces. The young men ate 15 ounces. That was 50 percent more than they ate the day before. Researchers say this is the problem with super-sized meals. People eat more because there is more on their plate.

when I get home, I get mad at my mom. I am mean to my little sister. I call her names that the kids call me. And she cries. Then I feel even more worthless. I'm fat and mean.[28]

Some fat teens hurt themselves, too. They take dangerous risks. They begin to use drugs or drink alcohol. Some even use knives or razors to cut themselves. "I did that for awhile," says one girl. "Not anymore, because I got help. But I would come home from school and cut my arms. It hurt, but I didn't care. Back then, I really hated myself."[29]

Other teens turn to food as a comfort. "It sounds funny," says one obese teen. "Food is a drug for me. I eat when I'm angry or upset. It

doesn't matter that I'm not hungry. I eat to comfort myself."

She says that she eats two or three times as much on bad days. "I go through McDonald's drive-through. That would be a day when people were really mean at school. So I order everything —I mean $20 or more worth of junk food. I eat in my car. No one can see me. And while I'm eating, I feel better. I've heard people on TV who do that too. There was a lady on *Oprah* who did that. She said food was her only friend. I totally get that."

She shakes her head. "What a stupid life I have, right?"[30]

What Can Be Done?

The number of overweight people in America is rising. It is important to solve this problem. Experts may not all agree on the best solution. But they do agree that the problem of obesity begins early. Pediatricians in the United States are very worried. Their organization calls obesity "the most common medical condition of childhood."[31] More than 80 percent of fat children become fat adults. This has to change soon, say doctors.

Surgery?

Some solutions target people who are already very heavy. Many of these people have had no luck with diets. They are so heavy that their health is at risk. Surgery has been one option for some of them. Doctors actually make the stomach smaller. They use special staples to close off most of the stomach. When they are finished, it is the size of an egg. The idea is that the patient will feel full quickly. In fact, eating six grapes will feel like a huge meal. After surgery the patient cannot overeat.

Recently some teens have been having the surgery, too. That worries some experts. They say the surgery is for adults. They do not know whether it is safe for a young person. But some teens are dangerously fat. They want the surgery, too.

Eric is a teen from South Carolina. He weighed 385 pounds (174.6kg). He had many health problems. He could not exercise, because he was too fat. His doctor believed Eric would have heart problems soon. He had the surgery. Now he weighs 190 pounds (86kg). It was a risk, he says, but he is glad he did it. "I was going to die from

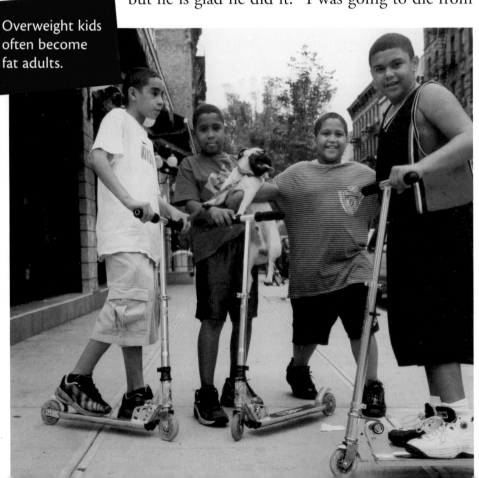

Overweight kids often become fat adults.

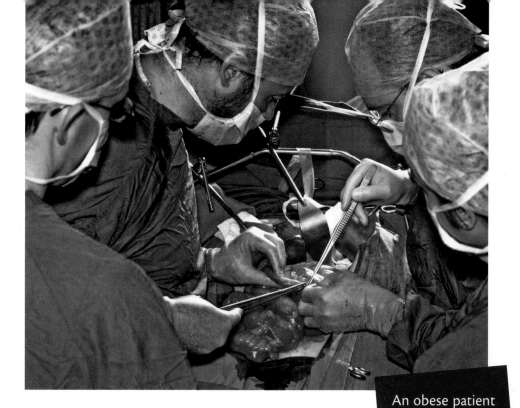

An obese patient has part of his stomach stapled shut.

being obese," he says. "I never want to go back to the way I was."[32]

No More Mocking

There are less severe ways to help at-risk teens who are too fat. One is to make schools just for them. One such school is in Fresno, California. It is called Academy of the Sierras. It is a regular high school, but students live there. There is one other big difference. Every student is obese. The school not only educates the teens. It helps them lose weight.

There are strict rules at the school. There are no computers or TVs in the dorm rooms. Students must eat healthy foods. They must exercise each day. They also have group therapy. In these sessions, they share experiences. They also discuss the best ways to keep off the pounds.

Even though the school is strict, the students love it. They are not teased or mocked. Jamie is a student at the school. She is 5 feet 2 inches (1.57m) and weighs 207 pounds (94kg). At her old school people called her names because of her weight. But that does not happen at this school. "There's no teasing here," she says. "We're all the same."[33]

Other towns are planning similar schools. Many students say they would love to attend one. "It's a great idea," says Jillian, an Oklahoma teen. "I'd love to be somewhere where they don't laugh. You could just concentrate on learning. You wouldn't have to feel bad all the time."[34]

Obese youths eat healthy food at the Academy of the Sierras.

Dogging It

Some exercise gets results easily. Researchers at the University of Missouri did an experiment. They assembled a group of obese adults. They gave each adult a dog from the animal shelter. The people were told to walk their dogs. At first they had to walk only ten minutes, three days a week. The time gradually increased. Eventually they walked twenty minutes, five days a week.

The results were amazing. The people had not dieted. They were eating the same foods as before. But the dog walking made a difference. In less than one year, the average person lost 14 pounds (6.4kg).

Attack the Snacks

Some solutions focus on prevention instead. One way is to help children make better food choices. For example, many parents hand out the wrong types of snacks. Many of the snacks are filled with sugar and other things that make children fat. They have too many calories without anything healthy.

"We've got to train parents," says Dr. Rob Larson. "If you give a toddler a cookie, do you expect her to refuse? No, of course not. Cookies taste great. But a cookie isn't the best choice. Parents need to rethink the idea of snacks."[35]

Other experts agree. One Texas doctor says children get too many snacks. He says they are

Teens snack on junk food.

handed out for the wrong reasons. He sees parents give snacks "the minute a child is upset, bored, or tired."[36] That is the wrong way to use any food, he says. Hunger is the only reason to eat.

School Lunches

Some schools are finding solutions in the lunchroom. Schools usually relied on pizza, hamburgers, and french fries. "Not the healthiest," admits Norah, a lunch worker in a junior high. "But it's what the kids want. If we served salads, kids probably would go hungry."[37]

But some schools are changing. They have hired chefs. Instead of the usual menu, the chefs experimented with new ideas. Jimmy Gherardi was hired by a school in Ohio. He made some changes right away. "The first thing we did," he says, "was throw the deep fryer away."[38]

Gherardi used less fats and oils. He used more fresh fruits and vegetables. But he made foods the students really liked. He served pizza. But it had whole-grain crust, which is very healthy. He made muffins that were healthy, too. He even made a

Disney and Happy Meals

For ten years the Walt Disney Company had a deal with McDonald's. Disney would make a children's movie. Then McDonald's would create a Happy Meal for children. The meal would have a toy based on the movie. McDonald's did this for many movies such as *Cars* and *Pirates of the Caribbean*. The deal made the Disney company a lot of money. McDonald's paid $1 billion each year to use the Disney characters.

But the Disney company was worried about obesity. They did not want to encourage young children to eat fast food. So Disney canceled the deal. McDonald's can no longer sell Happy Meals based on Disney movies.

The Food Pyramid

The U.S. Department of Agriculture has created a food pyramid to help you eat a healthy diet. Exercise is important, too.

MyPyramid.gov
STEPS TO A HEALTHIER YOU

Match the colors in the pyramid to the boxes below.

MEAT & BEANS

Get protein from low-fat or lean meats and poultry— baked, broiled, or grilled. Also eat fish, beans and nuts.

GRAINS

Eat 6 ounces daily of bread, cereal, crackers and pasta. Half should be whole grain foods.

FRUITS

Eat a variety of fruits: fresh, frozen, canned. Go easy on fruit juices.

VEGETABLES

Vary your veggies. Eat more dark green and orange veggies, dry beans and peas.

MILK

Go low-fat or fat-free with calcium-rich foods like milk, cheese, and yogurt.

OILS

Make most of your fat sources from fish, nuts, and vegetable oils. Limit solid fats like butter, stick margarine, shortening, and lard.

To get a healthy diet designed just for you, visit the Web site below for the "My Pyramid Plan." Fill in your age, weight, and daily exercise level.

www.mypyramid.gov/mypyramid/index.aspx

Source: U.S. Department of Agriculture.

healthy double-chocolate cookie. His experiments seemed to work. Students loved the new food. They even asked for recipes to take home.

Edible Schoolyards

Some schools are even going further in fighting obesity. Martin Luther King Jr. Middle School is doing amazing things. It is located in Berkeley, California. At that school, students are growing their own food.

In 1997 a woman named Alice Waters had the idea. She owns a restaurant near the school. She went inside the school one day. She was disappointed in the lunches students ate. The school

Alice Waters (far right) created the "Edible Schoolyard" program.

An "Edible Schoolyard" class cooks food they have grown.

did not cook the lunches for the children. Instead, Taco Bell and Pizza Hut sold them fast food.

Waters wanted to see the children learn to eat better. Fast food creates fat bodies. So she began a new program at the school. She called it "The Edible Schoolyard." She helped the children start a large garden on the school grounds. She taught them about taking care of plants. She helped them buy seedlings. She showed them how to tend and harvest the plants. Finally she taught them how to make good food from what they grew.

Today the program is stronger than ever. Children spend 90 minutes each week in the school garden. They experiment with different kinds of tomatoes, herbs, and beans. They grow fruit. They learn new recipes, too. The food they eat is healthier. It will not make them fat. Best of all, the children are proud of what they have learned. Waters's idea has become famous. She wants all students to learn to grow and cook good food. She says, "I hope to reach every single child."[39]

Making Exercise Fun

Another way to fight obesity is more exercise. That is nothing new. Everyone knows that exercise is a way to lose weight. But so many people avoid it. Children, especially, need to be more active. "How to make it fun is the problem," says Bill. He works with overweight people, helping them get healthier. "The heavy kids don't like it. They aren't athletes. They aren't used to success playing games. They're used to being the last kid picked in gym class. So they have no fun playing sports."[40]

In team sports, overweight kids are often excluded by their peers.

Walking is great exercise for anyone who is overweight.

Some think the answer is health clubs. There are new sorts of clubs. They are just for overweight children and teens. These clubs have workout sessions. They also have nutrition classes. One club even offers $50 prizes for good attendance. In January 2006 such clubs had 1.8 million customers. Many think health clubs are the answer.

Others have a different idea. Bill thinks overweight people should learn different sports. He says:

> Not team sports. But sports people can do alone, by themselves. That way they don't have to play on a team. Walking, skating, skiing—these are good. So is swimming.

These are life sports. You can learn them as a kid. And you can do them until you're very old. They are good for you. But mostly, they're fun. You can do them with others. But you don't need to compete.[41]

Laws and Commercials

Exercise and healthy food help prevent obesity. But some think laws can help, too. They say there are too many commercials for junk food. Most are aimed at children. In fact, 70 percent of ads aimed at children are for food. "And it's not healthy food," complains Gillian. She has three children under six years old. "Watch a Saturday morning cartoon show. Every ad is for cookies or candy or sweet cereal."[42]

Many experts agree with Gillian. They say young children are unfair targets. They cannot tell the difference between the ads and the cartoons. Some countries ban commercials aimed at children. Many people want to do that in the United States, too.

They say it could help prevent children from getting fat.

"A Time Bomb"

Obesity is a difficult problem. There is not just one way to solve it. Experts may disagree on the

This super-sized car seat is for overweight toddlers.

various ways. But they all agree on one thing. It is a problem that is getting worse every day.

A Minnesota doctor is very worried. "I've seen a grade school girl who weighs 215 pounds. I have another patient. A sixteen-year-old who weighs more than 500 pounds. He can't even bathe himself. We've got to wake up. We've got to turn this around."[43]

Dr. Harold Goldstein is a California public health expert. He agrees America is in deep trouble. There are too many obese adults. There are too many overweight children. Many have serious health problems. "We are sitting on a time bomb," he says.[44]

Appendix

Body Mass Index Table for Adults

How to Use the BMI Table:
- Find the appropriate height in the left-hand column labeled **Height**.
- Move across to a given **Body Weight** (in pounds).
- The number at the top of the column is the **BMI** at that height and weight.

	Normal						Overweight					Obese										Extreme Obesity				
BMI	**19**	**20**	**21**	**22**	**23**	**24**	**25**	**26**	**27**	**28**	**29**	**30**	**31**	**32**	**33**	**34**	**35**	**36**	**37**	**38**	**39**	**40**	**41**	**42**	**43**	**44**
Height (inches)												Body Weight (pounds)														
59	94	99	104	109	114	119	124	128	133	138	143	148	153	158	163	168	173	178	183	188	193	198	203	208	212	217
60	97	102	107	112	118	123	128	133	138	143	148	153	158	163	168	174	179	184	189	194	199	204	209	215	220	225
61	100	106	111	116	122	127	132	137	143	148	153	158	164	169	174	180	185	190	195	201	206	211	217	222	227	232
62	104	109	115	120	126	131	136	142	147	153	158	164	169	175	180	186	191	196	202	207	213	218	224	229	235	240
63	107	113	118	124	130	135	141	146	152	158	163	169	175	180	185	191	197	203	208	214	220	225	231	237	242	248
64	110	116	122	128	134	140	145	151	157	163	169	174	180	186	192	197	204	209	215	221	227	232	238	244	250	256
65	114	120	126	132	138	144	150	156	162	168	174	180	185	192	198	204	210	216	222	228	234	240	246	252	258	264
66	118	124	130	136	142	148	155	161	167	173	179	186	192	198	204	210	215	223	229	235	241	247	253	260	266	272
67	121	127	134	140	146	153	159	166	172	178	185	191	198	204	211	217	223	230	236	242	249	255	261	268	274	280
68	125	131	138	144	151	158	164	171	177	184	190	197	203	210	216	223	230	236	243	249	256	262	269	276	282	289
69	128	135	142	149	155	162	169	176	182	189	196	203	209	216	223	230	236	243	250	257	263	270	277	284	291	297
70	132	139	146	153	160	167	174	181	185	195	202	209	216	222	229	236	243	250	257	264	271	278	285	292	299	306
71	136	143	150	157	165	172	179	186	193	200	206	215	222	229	236	243	250	257	265	272	279	286	293	301	308	315
72	140	147	154	162	169	177	184	191	199	206	213	221	228	235	242	250	258	265	272	279	287	294	302	309	316	324
73	144	151	159	166	174	182	189	197	204	212	219	227	235	242	250	257	265	272	280	288	295	302	310	318	325	333
74	148	155	163	171	179	186	194	202	210	218	225	233	241	249	256	264	272	280	287	295	303	311	319	326	334	342
75	152	160	166	176	184	192	200	206	216	224	232	240	248	256	264	272	279	287	295	303	311	319	327	335	343	351

BMI is not always an accurate indicator of health, since people are not identical. Your doctor is your best source of information on weight issues.

This BMI Table is not accurate for children, pregnant or nursing women, very muscular people, or endurance athletes. Additional research may be needed for better accuracy in people over 65 years of age.

Source: www.nhlbi.nih.gov/guidelines/obesity/bmi_tbl.htm. Adapted from *Clinical Guidelines on the Identification, Evaluation, and Treatment of Overweight and Obesity in Adults: The Evidence Report.*

Notes

Introduction: A Land of Fat People

1. Rusty, personal interview, October 30, 2006, Blaine, MN.
2. Jillian, personal interview, November 2, 2006, Minneapolis, MN.
3. Connie, telephone interview, October 30, 2006.

Chapter 1: How Did America Get So Fat?

4. Bill, personal interview, October 23, 2006, Edina, MN.
5. Jeri, personal interview, October 28, 2006, Saint Paul, MN.
6. Martin, personal interview, October 24, 2006, Minneapolis, MN.
7. Trina, personal interview, September 11, 2006, Minneapolis, MN.
8. Quoted in "Should Kids Skip Gym Class?" *Current Events*, April 26, 2002, p. 3.
9. Quoted in "Should Kids Skip Gym Class?" p. 3.
10. Bill, personal interview.

11. Trina, personal interview.
12. Gavin, telephone interview, November 5, 2006.
13. Mac, personal interview, October 23, 2006, Richfield, MN.
14. Bill, personal interview.

Chapter 2: The Dangers of Being Fat

15. Bill, personal interview.
16. Rusty, personal interview.
17. Connie, telephone interview.
18. Connie, telephone interview.
19. Dr. Rob Larson, personal interview, November 13, 2006, Minneapolis, MN.

Chapter 3: Fat on the Inside

20. Corrine, telephone interview, November 14, 2006.
21. Debbie, personal interview, October 20, 2006, Minneapolis, MN.
22. Quoted in Dara R. Musher-Eizenman and Shayla Holub, "What Young Children Think of Overweight Individuals," *Pediatrics for Parents*, October 2004, p. 5.
23. Quoted in Alexis Jetter, "Don't Hate Me Because I'm Fat," *Good Housekeeping*, October 2005, p. 186.
24. Quoted in *Current Events*, "Operation Obesity: Surgery for Overweight Teens a

Weighty Matter," December 10, 2004, p. 3.

25. Name withheld, personal interview, October 17, 2006, Minneapolis, MN.
26. Jillian, personal interview.
27. Quoted in "Too Wide to Ride," *Men's Fitness*, August 2004, p. 78.
28. Sharri, personal interview, November 8, 2006, Mankato, MN.
29. Marci, personal interview, January 14, 1997, Saint Paul, MN.
30. Name withheld, personal interview.

Chapter 4: What Can Be Done?

31. Quoted in Amanda Spake, "The Future of Fatness," *U.S. News & World Report*, February 9, 2004, p. 56.
32. Quoted in *Current Events*, "Operation Obesity," p. 3.
33. Quoted in Allison Adato, "Class Size," *People*, October 25, 2004, p. 125.
34. Jillian, personal interview.
35. Larson, personal interview.
36. Quoted in Robert A. Barnett, "Why You Need to Change Your Child's Snacking Habits," *Parenting*, September 1, 2005, p. 122.
37. Norah, personal interview, November 9, 2006, Minneapolis, MN.
38. Quoted in Ted Kreiter, "Stealth Health," *Saturday Evening Post*, March/April 2006, p. 82.

39. Quoted in Umut Newbery, "Teaching Kids About Real Food," *Mother Earth News*, December 2004–January 2005, p. 24.
40. Bill, personal interview.
41. Bill, personal interview.
42. Gillian, personal interview, November 9, 2006, Minneapolis, MN.
43. Steven, telephone interview, November 2, 2006.
44. Quoted in Jill Smolowe, "Everything to Lose," *People*, November 4, 2002, p. 58.

Glossary

amputate: To cut off or remove.

cartilage: A material between the bones of a joint, such as a knee or shoulder.

diabetes: A disease that can be life threatening. It is common among overweight people.

epidemic: A medical emergency that is widespread.

glucose: Sugar the body produces from food.

insulin: A chemical the body makes to help glucose get into the cells.

obese: Severely overweight.

pediatrician: A doctor who cares for babies and children.

portion: The amount of food in a single serving.

sleep apnea: A condition in which people temporarily stop breathing during sleep.

Bibliography

Books

Charlene Akers, *Obesity*. San Diego: Lucent, 2000. Good section on the ways doctors treat obese patients.

Laura Buller, *Food*. New York: DK, 2005. A complete examination of healthy foods and how good eating can prevent certain diseases.

Ann Cooper and Lisa Holmes, *Lunch Lessons: Changing the Way We Feed Our Children*. New York: HarperCollins, 2006. Recipes and information about how parents could help children and teens eat better.

Scott Ingram, *Want Fries with That? Obesity and the Supersizing of America*. New York: Franklin Watts, 2005. Very readable, with helpful index.

Joanna Kedge, *Diet*. Chicago: Raintree, 2005. Interesting information on eating disorders, special diets, and obesity. Good bibliography.

Gail B. Stewart, *Diabetes*. San Diego: KidHaven, 2003. Easy reading, with information about complications from the disease.

Periodicals

Natalie Kusz, "The Fat Lady Sings," *O, the Oprah Magazine*, August 2002.

Michael D. Lemonick, "How We Grew So Big," *Time*, June 7, 2004.

Cathy Newman, "Why Are We So Fat?" *National Geographic*, August 2004.

Web Sites

American Obesity Association (www.obesity.org). This site has information on childhood obesity. It explains the BMI index and talks about health problems associated with obesity.

Edible Schoolyard (www.edibleschoolyard.org/ homepage.html). Information about Alice Waters and her program in a Berkeley, California, school.

I Was a Fat Kid . . . This Is My Story (www. catay. com/fatkid/index.asp). Stories told by young and old people who were fat. Many are painful to read, but very helpful.

"Overweight and Obesity," Centers for Disease Control and Prevention (www.cdc.gov/nccdphp/ dnap/obesity). This site explains the various medical risks of being overweight.

Index